See how they grow

Farm

DK

Duckling

My mother has laid her eggs in this nest.
Inside each egg, a duckling is growing.
One of them is me!

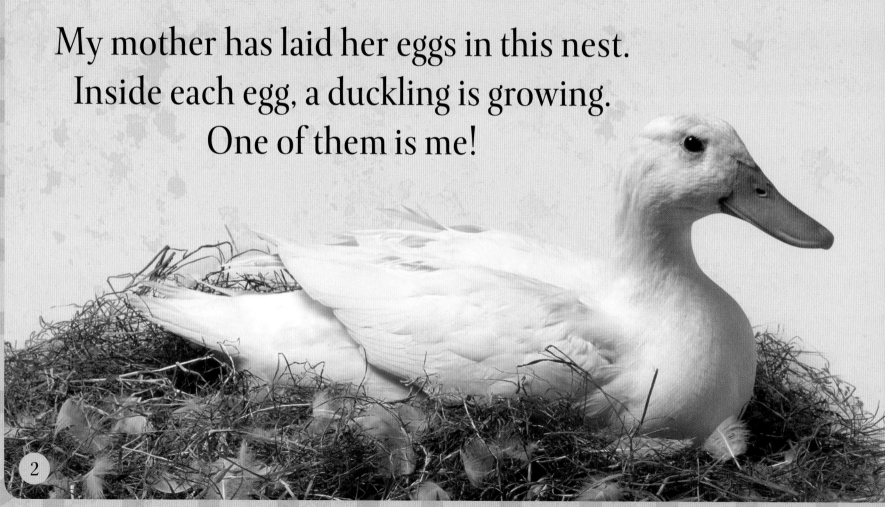

When I'm ready to hatch, I slowly peck my way out of the shell. It's tiring work for a little duckling like me!

Starting to hatch

Halfway out

Almost there

When my downy feathers are dry, I stand up and look for food. I'm only two days old but I can walk, and cheep too.

One hour

Two days

Seven days

Soon my soft yellow down is replaced by white feathers. At six weeks old, I'm all grown up.

Three weeks

Six weeks

Chick

This is my mother.
She is sitting on her
eggs to keep them
warm and safe.

I am one of the chicks growing inside an egg.
I start to chip around the inside of my
eggshell. I push the shell apart.
Phew! At last I am free.

Hatching   Pushing through   Newly hatched chick

My feathers have dried and now they are soft and fluffy. I am hungry, so I find some seeds to peck. It's not long before new feathers grow on my wings.

A few days

Eight days

Two weeks

I have a bright red comb on my head and a
wattle under my beak. I am big and strong.

Four weeks

Eight weeks

Piglet

I am a piglet. I have just been born. So have my brothers and sisters. My mum lies down and snorts when it's time for us to drink her milk.

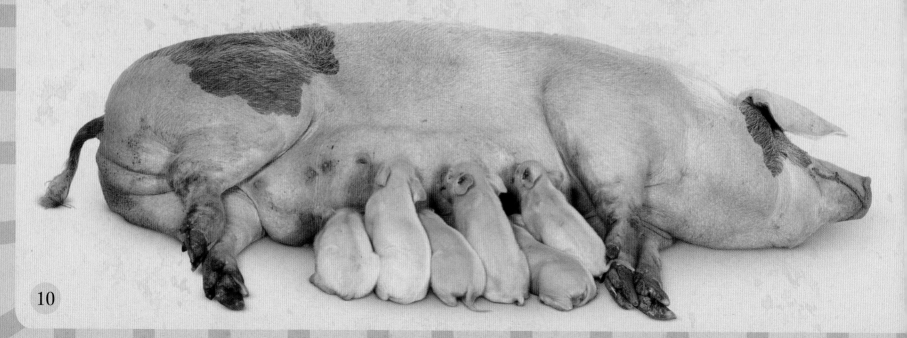

I can soon stand up and trot around.
I like to squeal. It's my way of saying,
"Hello, I want to be fed!"

Newborn

Two days

One week

My ears get bigger every day. I sniff around with my squishy snout, searching for things to eat.

Six weeks

Six months

I've grown up to be as big as my mum! Now I'm ready to have my own babies.

One year

13

Lamb

I am a newborn lamb.
I stay close to my mother.
I feel very sleepy.
My woolly coat keeps
me warm while I rest.

I bleat loudly when my mum goes away.
I can see and hear, but my legs are very weak.
Sometimes I fall, but I get straight back up.

Four hours

One day

I am four weeks old now. I'm growing up fast.
My fleecy coat is getting thicker. I like to run
and jump around in the field. What fun!

Four weeks

Eight weeks

I spend most of the day nibbling on fresh green grass. Soon I will be fully grown.

Ten weeks

Twelve weeks

Calf

I am a calf. I have just been born. My mother moos softly to me.

I am trying to stand up but my legs are wobbly. It won't be long, though, before I'm strong enough to walk.

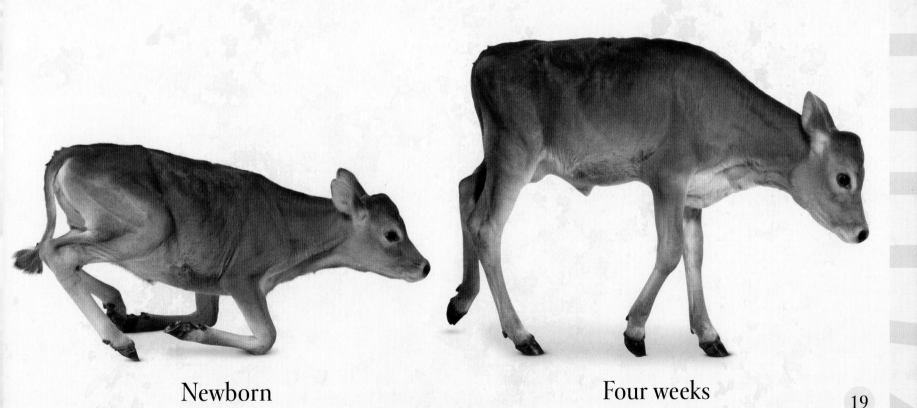

Newborn

Four weeks

My winter coat is thick and velvety.
I enjoy eating grass all day long.

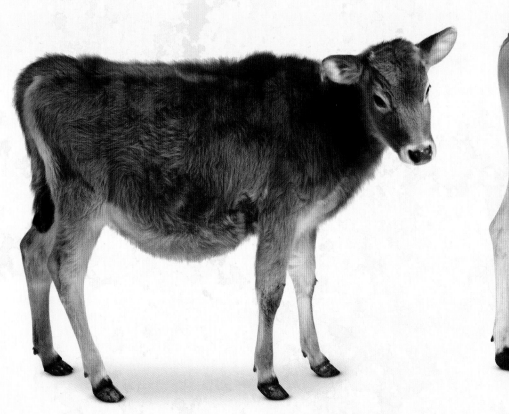

Five months

Ten months

My coat is changing colour and I am starting to look like the big cows. Soon I will have a calf of my own.

Fourteen months

How did they grow?

Duckling

Chick

22

Piglet

Lamb

Calf

Penguin Random House

Editor Sally Beets
Senior Editor Roohi Sehgal
Assistant Editor Niharika Prabhakar
Project Art Editor Jaileen Kaur
Designer Charlotte Jennings
Jacket Designers Rachael Hare, Dheeraj Arora
Jacket Co-ordinator Issy Walsh
DTP Designers Sachin Gupta, Vijay Kandwal
Picture Researcher Vagisha Pushp
Production Editor Abi Maxwell
Production Controller Basia Ossowska
Managing Editors Jonathan Melmoth, Monica Saigal
Managing Art Editors Diane Peyton Jones,
Romi Chakraborty
Delhi Creative Heads Glenda Fernandes,
Malavika Talukder
Publishing Manager Francesca Young
Creative Director Helen Senior
Publishing Director Sarah Larter

First published in Great Britain in 2021 by
Dorling Kindersley Limited
One Embassy Gardens, 8 Viaduct Gardens,
London, SW11 7BW

Copyright © 2021 Dorling Kindersley Limited
A Penguin Random House Company
10 9 8 7 6 5 4 3 2 1
001–321695–Feb/2021

A CIP catalogue record for this book
is available from the British Library.
ISBN: 978-0-2414-6747-3

Printed and bound in China

For the curious
www.dk.com

ACKNOWLEDGEMENTS

The publisher would like to thank the following for their kind permission
to reproduce their photographs:
(Key: a-above; b-below/bottom; c-centre; f-far; l-left; r-right; t-top)

1 Dorling Kindersley: Barrie Watts / (cl). **2 Dorling Kindersley:** Barrie Watts (b).
3 Dorling Kindersley: Barrie Watts (bl, bc, br). **4 Dorling Kindersley:** Barrie Watts
(bl, bc, br). **5 Dorling Kindersley:** Barrie Watts (bl, br). **17 123RF.com:** robertsrob (bc).
22 Dorling Kindersley: Barrie Watts / (cl, c/Duckling, c, cr).
22–23 Dreamstime.com: Galina Drokina (x20)

Endpaper images: *Front:* **Dorling Kindersley:** Barrie Watts bl;
Back: **Dorling Kindersley:** Barrie Watts bl

Cover images: *Front:* **Dorling Kindersley:** Barrie Watts c; **Dreamstime.com:**
Galina Drokina; *Back:* **Dorling Kindersley:** Barrie Watts fcla, cla, tc/ (Yellow), tc, tr;
Dreamstime.com: Galina Drokina; *Spine:* **Dorling Kindersley:** Barrie Watts

All other images © Dorling Kindersley
For further information see: www.dkimages.com

MIX
Paper from
responsible sources
FSC™ C018179

This book was made with Forest Stewardship
Council™ certified paper – one small step in DK's
commitment to a sustainable future. For more
information go to www.dk.com/our-green-pledge